Helping Your Baby to Sleep

an easy-to-follow guide

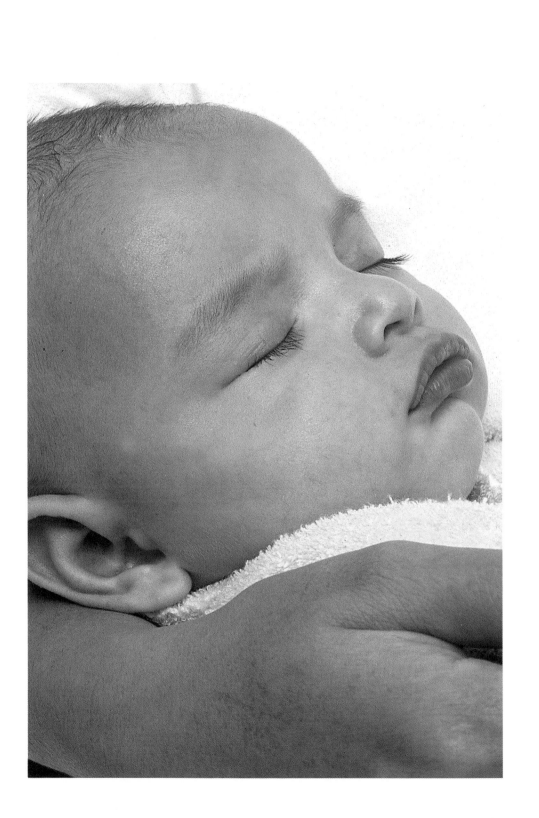

Helping Your Baby to Sleep

an easy-to-follow guide

Siobhan Mulholland

Vermilion

Contents

Introduction

It will be some time before your baby fits in with your sleeping pattern, but be assured, as he gets older, it will become more similar. He will learn the difference between daytime and night-time, how to sleep for more than two hours in one go, and how to fall asleep without an all singing, all dancing performance from you.

As with most aspects of child development, how a baby behaves is a mixture of nature and nurture. As he gets older, your baby should sleep for longer stretches of time at night – some of this will happen naturally, some of it will be with your help.

Here you will learn what happens when your baby sleeps, how to get him to sleep, and how to help him stay asleep. It is true that some babies find all this a lot easier than others. But remember only a few babies have a genuine sleep disorder; the vast majority are capable of sleeping through a big chunk of the night by six months old.

Please note that to avoid confusion the baby has always been referred to as 'he' but this could just as easily have been 'she'.

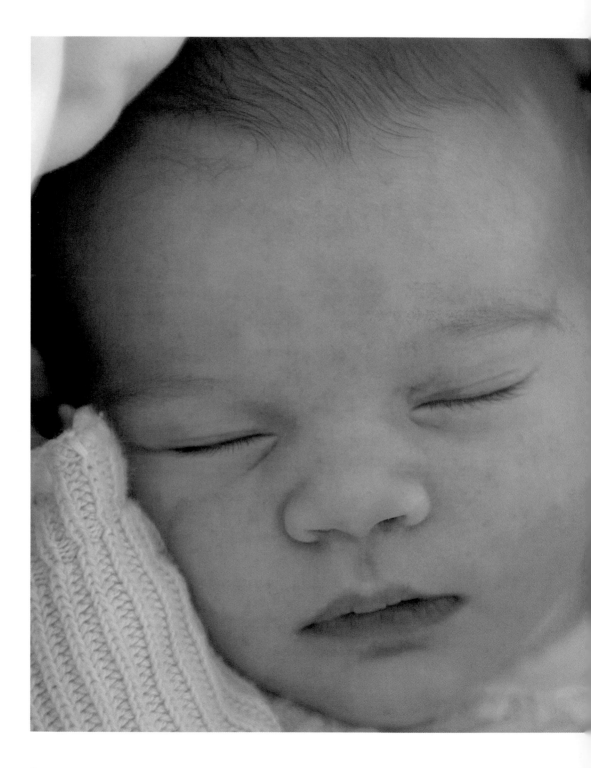

Chapter 1

SLEEP What you need to know

So why is sleep so important? There are many theories, but the overall reason why remains a mystery. What the scientists are certain about is that having an adequate amount of sleep is important – especially for babies and children. It is vital for development, growth, memory and learning. It's also restorative: it helps us recover from being awake and sets us up well for the next day. After all, it's not just the young who get 'cranky' if they don't get enough sleep. It affects the way we think and function, our moods and behaviour. It's so important that if we 'lose' sleep, if we have a bad night, our bodies make up for it by sleeping longer and more intensely the next night.

What happens during sleep

A lot goes on while we sleep – we are not cut off from the outside world. The amount of light in the room, a change in temperature or in noise levels, it all has an effect on us while we are asleep. We are conscious of our environment and impulses: if we are too hot or too cold, whether we are hungry or uncomfortable. This is because sleep is an active, organised physiological process. Our eyes may be shut, our bodies lying down but there's still a lot going on.

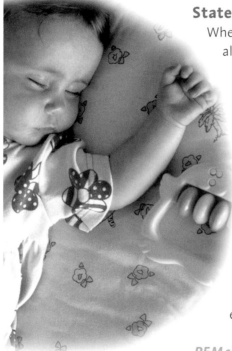

States of sleep

When we sleep we all – babies and adults alike – experience different types and depths of sleep. These are categorised into two distinct states: 'light' sleep and 'deep' sleep – also known as REM sleep (Rapid Eye Movement sleep) and non-REM sleep (non-Rapid Eye Movement sleep). During the night we move between the two – from light sleep to deep sleep and back again in cycles. For your baby, these patterns of sleep will have started to evolve in the womb during the last months of your pregnancy. REM sleep develops at about seven months and non-REM at around eight months in unborn babies.

REM sleep: this is the state of sleep closest to wakefulness. In babies it is referred to as 'active sleep'. Your baby will have experienced more REM in the month before he was born than he will at any other time during his life. At birth, REM makes up 50 per cent of total sleep: around 8– 10 hours a day. In the first year of life, this figure drops rapidly. By the time your baby is 12 months old, he will be experiencing around five hours of REM sleep over a 24-hour period. It will still be quite a while before he catches up with you, though, as adults only experience around 100 minutes of REM sleep a night.

While in REM sleep we are more 'vigilant', more conscious of what's going on.

We wake up more easily in this state of sleep. You are likely to wake up because of certain, specific noises; whereas your baby is likely to wake up because of hunger or discomfort. During this state of sleep your baby is developing and growing all the time, in the same way as he does when he's awake.

What happens when your baby experiences REM sleep:

● Your baby's eyelids will be closed but his eyes will appear to dart from side to side beneath their lids. Even adults experiencing REM sleep can occasionally be seen to move their eyes back and forth beneath their eyelids. (Which explains the name Rapid Eye Movement.)

● Your baby may smile, frown or twitch.

● Up until six months of age your baby's body may jerk while he is asleep and he might even make the odd sound. The younger your baby is the more likely this will happen; as he matures and develops these movements will lessen.

● Your baby's breathing and heartbeat will become irregular.

● Your baby uses up more energy and oxygen while in 'active' sleep.

● He may have more difficulty trying to regulate his temperature in this state of sleep.

● This is when older children and adults dream, so your baby may be dreaming as well; but as babies can't tell us we don't know for sure.

● 80 per cent of a premature baby's total sleep is made up of REM sleep *(see page 56)*.

Non-REM sleep: this stage is sometimes referred to as 'quiet' sleep in babies. During this stage your baby will:

● Have that angelic, peaceful look on his face.

● Breathe deeply and lie very still.

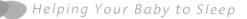

● Only twitch or jerk occasionally.

● Have a more regular heartbeat.

● Be difficult to wake up.

We know from older children and adults that no dreaming happens during this state. Non-REM sleep is divided up into a further four stages varying from drowsiness to very deep sleep. Your baby will not fully experience these stages until he is around six months old.

Stage 1: your baby will experience the lightest sleep – it's the in-between stage when he's half awake and half asleep. He may be drowsy, and his eyes may droop and slowly close.

Stage 2: your baby will be asleep, but it's still a very light sleep. He will be quiet and not move; his breathing pattern and heart rate will start to slow. He can still be awakened easily, so if there's a sudden, loud noise it will startle him and he may jump.

Stage 3: your baby will be in a very deep sleep and will not move.

Stage 4: your baby's breathing and heart rate will be at their lowest levels because he will be in a truly deep sleep. It will be difficult to wake him, so you won't have to tip-toe around and keep noise levels to a minimum.

Sleep cycles

Your sleep 'cycle' comes round every 90 minutes, but for your baby it happens every 50 minutes. As a newborn, he will start off his cycle by going straight into REM sleep; he won't adopt the more adult pattern (of entering non-REM sleep first, followed by REM and then back again) until he is three months old.

The fact that your baby has a more rapid sleep cycle is significant because at the end of each cycle, as we move from non-REM sleep to REM, we wake up slightly – we undergo a moment of arousal. For most of us this is not a problem: we don't wake up all the way and then we fall asleep again easily without remembering this brief period of wakefulness. But it's different for your baby: not only do these moments of wakefulness come around much more frequently

OUR BODY CLOCK

As well as sleep patterns, we also have an internal body clock, which tells us when to go to bed and when to get up in the morning. This clock controls our 'circadian rhythm' – the times each day when we release hormones that make us sleepy, alert and hungry. The clock is set using cues such as sunlight and darkness. Put simply: when it's light we feel awake and when it's dark we start to get sleepy. In adults it runs on an approximately 24-hour cycle, making us fall asleep at night and wake up the next morning. Your baby is born with this clock, but it needs to be regulated and synchronised with everyone else's

but he also has to learn the falling-back-to-sleep-easily trick.

So when your baby is under three months old you have a bit of a double whammy. Not only does he experience much more 'light' sleep than an older child, from which he coud easily be awakened, but his sleep cycles are also shorter, bringing even more opportunities for waking up.

However, as your newborn baby matures so does his sleep cycle. His cycle will grow longer and he will experience less REM sleep, so – with maybe a little help from you – he should wake up less frequently as he gets older.

How much sleep your baby needs

How much your baby sleeps, especially for the first few days after his birth, is to a certain extent out of your control. He will have as much sleep as he needs, whenever he needs it, wherever he is. There is not a lot you can do about this as it's very difficult to keep a sleepy baby awake, or make a well-rested baby go to sleep. However, it may be reassuring to know that it is

AVERAGE NUMBER OF HOURS OF SLEEP

	Total Night Time Sleep	Total Daytime Sleep
1 Week	Approximately 16 hours spread over a 24 hour period	
1 Month	14 – 15 hours spread over a 24 hour period	
3 Months	$8\frac{1}{2}$ - 10 hours	$4\frac{1}{2}$ - 5 hours
6 Months	$9\frac{1}{2}$ - 11 hours	2 - 4 hours
9 Months	$9\frac{1}{2}$ - 11 Hours	$2\frac{1}{2}$ - 3
12 Months	$9\frac{1}{2}$ - $11\frac{1}{2}$ hours	$1\frac{1}{2}$ - $2\frac{1}{2}$ hours
18 Months	$9\frac{1}{2}$ - $11\frac{1}{2}$	2 hours

impossible for a newborn baby to get too much sleep.

When calculating the length of time your baby sleeps, it does not include any 'settling down time' – that is, the time from when he is placed in his cot to when he actually falls asleep. It also does not include the time your baby spends awake in his cot before you pick him up in the morning, or after a nap *(see page 17)*.

A rough guide: the figures shown in the chart *(see above)* are indicators, not exact measures, of the number of hours babies of different ages sleep. It's a bit like asking how long a piece of string is: every baby is different and the amount of hours they sleep, and need, varies widely. In the same way that adults have varying sleep needs, so do babies. Some adults can get away with five hours' sleep a night, others need eight or nine. With newborn babies the average number of hours spent sleeping over a 24-hour period is 16, but some babies will sleep for as few as 10 hours during this period and others for twice as long as that – as many as 20 hours. It really is the luck of the draw.

It's also worth remembering that as your baby grows, his sleeping pattern will change very fast *(see pages 13– 16)*. You might start out with a baby who is a 'good sleeper' – one that sleeps a lot and easily. Then, several weeks later, you could suddenly find yourself with a very wakeful baby: the type who only sleeps in fits and starts, and, compared with other babies of the same age, not that often.

Your baby's sleep patterns

Your baby will have no problem letting you know if he hasn't had enough sleep. A tired baby is irritable, fussy and cries a lot. If he's had as much sleep as he needs, he will be 'well rested'. This means that he will wake spontaneously, feed well, be alert and appear content.

0–2 months: your newborn baby will sleep in short, sharp bursts – maybe for as little as one hour at a time, rarely longer than about three hours. When he sleeps and for how long he sleeps will be unpredictable, but what you can usually rely on is him being asleep more often than he is awake. His sleep will seem like a series of naps which occur throughout the day and night. He will wake up often because he is hungry: infants this young have very small stomachs – no larger than the size of their fist. Your newborn baby will need feeding 'little and often' and after each feed he is likely to fall straight back to sleep again. It's a simple equation at this age: an empty tummy will make your baby wake up, while a full one will make him sleep.

What is important with newborns is that they do not go any longer than 3–4 hours between feeds. If your baby is asleep, but needs to be fed, wake him gently and make sure he feeds. Premature babies need to feed even more often – your health visitor will be able to guide you.

3–5 months: by three months your baby's sleep pattern will have developed significantly, so he should rouse less often while he sleeps. Sleep will have started to become a distinct activity for your baby, no longer necessarily associated with his next feed. As your baby's tummy grows, he will be able to last longer between feeds. He will now understand the difference between night and day: he will be more awake and active during the day between his naps *(see page 28)* and he will sleep at night.

A pattern will start to emerge for the times when your baby wakes up and goes to sleep. Life starts to become a little more predictable as he discovers his own rhythms. He may start having 3, maybe 4 naps a day – say one long nap in the morning and two shorter ones in the afternoon. At night he might be able to 'sleep through', perhaps for an unbroken stretch of sleep that lasts five or six hours, sometimes more. This long period of sleep usually starts after a late-night feed and lasts until the early morning – from say midnight until 5am. This will happen earlier for bottle-fed babies (at around 10 weeks) than for breastfed babies (at around 13 weeks). When your baby is this age, you may be asked if he has 'settled' yet – this is another way of asking if he is 'sleeping through'.

6–8 months: by six months your baby's longest period of sleep will be at night, lasting $9\frac{1}{2}$–11 hours, although he will probably wake at least once during this time. He is certainly physiologically capable of 'sleeping through the night' now, for a stretch of 6–8 hours in one go. If he manages to sleep for longer without disturbing you, then you are fortunate, you have a baby who really has worked out how to settle himself to sleep without your help. At this age babies no longer need to be fed during the night. This is when they start on solid food and as long as they are getting enough nourishment during the day there should be no need for any midnight snacking. Your baby's daytime sleep will probably consist of two, sometimes three, naps a day. But just when you think you

TOP TIP

As your baby develops he will give you more clues as to when he is tired and ready for sleep. As well as being irritable and fussy he may start yawning or rubbing his eyes. He may have difficulty focusing on you, or he may try to bury his head in your chest. He may also try to seek comfort by trying to suck on something.

are there with this sleeping lark – that you have a good sleeper who is sleeping for large chunks of the night – you might find that your baby starts waking up for lots of other reasons which have nothing to do with being fed. At this age babies go through a bit of a growth spurt, one that may cause night waking. At the same time, your baby is developing socially and emotionally. He may start showing signs of 'separation anxiety', becoming distressed when you leave him and behaving more 'clingy' than usual (see page 43). This can prolong your bedtime routine or cause problems when settling your baby back to sleep.

Your baby's sleep may also be disturbed by the onset of teething (see page 42), which can cause discomfort. At this age your baby may discover the ability to roll over, to move around in his cot, knocking into the sides and waking himself up in the process.

9–11 months: by nine months, there will have been a big shift in the balance of your baby's night-time and daytime sleeping. He will be very clear about the difference between the two. He will be sleeping for $9^1/_2$–11 hours a night , but will still be prone to night waking. If he hasn't done so already, this is when your baby may drop his late-afternoon nap and be very happy with just having one long nap a day. Some babies will still be having two short naps: one in the morning and one in the afternoon. Your baby's sleep patterns should now be very predictable, giving you more freedom to plan your day.

That said, this is again the age when some of the best sleepers start having 'sleep problems'. For instance, your baby might now be able to pull himself up with the help of the bars at the side of his cot. Getting back down again is a different thing, though, requiring frequent assistance from you in the middle of the night. Your baby may also need your help to find a lost teddy or dummy in those oh-so-early hours of the morning. This is also the age when some babies find for the first time that they need you by their side to help them go to sleep again.

12 months: by his first birthday, your baby will still need $9^1/_2$– $11^1/_2$ hours' sleep a night and one or two naps during the day. He might drop his morning nap, and just have one long nap after lunch each day. Because your baby is staying awake for longer stretches during the day and is much more active, you may find he is more ready for sleep at nap times and bedtime. However, his increased mobility might cause a problem when he is supposed to be lying down peacefully in his cot: at around one year old, be prepared for a lot of standing up and crying.

TOP TIP
Don't let your baby's last nap of the day be a late one. If he naps too near to bedtime he may not be ready to sleep again so soon after it.

AVERAGE NUMBER OF NAPS PER DAY

Age	Naps per day	Total Daytime Sleep
3 months	3-4	$4^1/_2$ - 5 hours
6 months	2-3	2 - 4 hours
9 months	2	$2^1/_2$ - 3 hours
12 months onwards	1-2	$1^1/_2$ - $2^1/_2$ hours

Naps

Your baby needs his daytime naps, and he will probably have at least one a day until he is three years old or so. How many naps he has per day, and at what time each day, changes dramatically during the course of his first year. With newborns, daytime naps and night-time sleep seem to all merge into one. But by three months your baby will have sorted out this difference with most of his sleeping occuring at night and three or more naps during the day. By around six months he'll probably be down to about two naps a day and any time from his first birthday onwards he might get by with just one big nap after lunch.

Getting the amount of daytime sleep right is a fine balance. Too much napping can lead to difficulties at bedtime: if a baby has slept too much in the day he will not settle well or sleep through the night. But having too little sleep during the day can also cause problems: an overtired baby easily becomes agitated and distressed and has difficulty settling to sleep.

Again not all babies are the same. Some will need to sleep more during the day, others less. Some will find it very difficult to cope if they miss a nap, whereas others will not appear any different. It's important that you do what seems right for your baby.

Chapter 2

HOW TO SETTLE YOUR BABY
Useful strategies

If your baby is tired and wants to sleep, he will sleep – that's not the difficult part. The tricky bit is trying to get your baby to sleep at the times you want him to, when it suits you, your family and everyone else – for instance, in the middle of the night or afternoon. It's something that can be done, but you need to provide pointers along the way, clues about when to sleep, signs which your baby will recognise even at a few weeks old.

A bedtime routine

This is probably the easiest place to start as it's a natural way to end each day. Your baby will learn, through your signs, that the pace has changed and it's time to wind down in preparation for sleep. A bedtime routine usually involves a bath or a wash, a nappy change, a story, a cuddle goodnight, into bed and then, hopefully, to sleep. The combination of what goes into the routine is up to you – there are no hard and fast rules about what has to happen and you can change the details as your baby gets older.

Through this regular sequence of events, your baby will learn that night follows day. He will come to associate 'bath, book, bed' with sleep and learn that what starts with moving into the bedroom area will always end with him being put down in his cot for the night.

TOP TIP

Stick to the same bedtime. The aim is for your baby to get into a rhythm and he can only do this when he's cottoned on to the fact that around a certain time of day he's meant to be asleep.

Introducing this routine: if you want, you can introduce this routine as soon as you bring your baby home. You don't have to include everything, just elements that suit you and your baby at that stage. You will need to give your baby a gentle cleanse or a bath once a day, so why not start off by doing this at the same time every day, at bedtime? After all, a routine like this is as much about helping parents as it is about setting up good sleep practices for your baby.

By the time he is three months old your baby will definitely be able to pick up on all these bedtime 'cues', so if you haven't done so before it's worth thinking about introducing a routine now. In the beginning this is best approached like one big rehearsal. It is an event that will not always run smoothly: on some days you'll want to give it a miss and on other days, despite your best efforts, your baby may well refuse to sleep. But do persevere – you will get there in the end.

Deciding on a bedtime: most parents opt to put their baby to bed at around six or seven o'clock in the evening. If your baby's needs can be made to fit in with yours and any older children in the family, then the whole thing will be much easier to pull off.

REPETITION, REPETITION, REPETITION.
What is important is that you do the same thing, in the same way, at roughly the same time every day. Each family will probably have a slightly different way of going about it, which is fine as long as they stick to it. Even if, at the beginning, you feel it's a lot of work for just a few hours' sleep, it is worth it: each time you do it your baby will be a step closer to learning what bedtime is all about.

How long it should take: the bedtime routine should be no more than 45 minutes and no less than 20 minutes. Too long, and your baby will become distracted, or maybe even fall asleep halfway through. Too short, and you'll be rushing, which your baby will pick up on and possibly become agitated by. Aim for around 30 minutes.

Winding down: there is no point introducing a 'wind down' to bedtime if your child is not ready for sleep. If he's had a nap *(see pages 16–17)* late in the day, which has left him refreshed and raring to go, it doesn't matter how good your routine is, it will not work.

- You want everything associated with the routine to be different from what's gone on before. To help your baby wind down, it can help to start in the bedroom area, which should be a place of peace and sleep.

- All the activities at this time of day should be low-key; keep stimulation to a minimum. For example, don't let your partner return home from work and upset the dynamic by roaring in and energetically greeting everyone.

- From just a few weeks old, babies understand differences in the tone of voices, so change your voice at bedtime.

TOP TIP
Try to enjoy this time yourself – it is a pleasurable and intimate moment between you and your baby.

TOP TIP
To further relax your baby before he goes to sleep you can try massaging him very gently. As long as the room and your hands are warm, your baby should enjoy it.

Start talking to your baby in a gentle, soothing manner, and mention that it's 'time for bed'. You'll be surprised how quickly he comes to understand the meaning of those words.

A wash, a change and a feed: when he is very young, your baby will not need a bath every day – perhaps just once or twice a week. Instead, he can be washed gently, which is often referred to as 'topping and tailing'. By about 4–6 weeks you will find your baby really comes to enjoy time spent splashing about in a warm bath and being wrapped up in cosy towels. After his wash, put a clean nappy and sleepsuit on your baby, then give him his last feed in the room he will be sleeping in. From around six weeks, try not to let him fall asleep during this feed. It's best to attempt to settle your baby while he's still awake. This will help him learn how to get to sleep on his own without your help *(see page 33)*. And finally, give him a big kiss and cuddle goodnight.

Where your baby sleeps

Where a baby sleeps was until recently a matter of personal choice. Mums and dads chose what suited them and their way of parenting. However, fears of 'cot death' have made everyone question their choices. Sudden Infant Death Syndrome (SIDS) is when a baby dies unexpectedly for unknown reasons, often while asleep in his cot. Babies under six months are most vulnerable.

Although cot death is rare, The Foundation for the Study of Infant Deaths *(see page 62)* recommends various things you can do to minimise the risk. For instance, they believe it is safer for babies under six months old to sleep in a cot in their parents' bedroom. This means you are more likely to be on hand should your baby get into difficulty. Like many parents, you may prefer this option anyway as having your baby so close makes it a lot easier to cope with night-time waking, when your baby needs feeding and comforting.

When your baby is older, it might then be a good idea to move him to a different room and listen to him through a baby monitor. If you find that every infant snuffle and snort keeps you awake, this is perhaps a welcome option.

Moses baskets and cots

Many babies start off sleeping in a Moses basket, which is cosy, snug and easily portable. It should not be used to transport your baby outside the home, but it can be moved around the house for daytime naps and night-time sleep. The baskets do not take up a lot of room, so your baby can sleep in one next to your bed – either on the floor, or on a stand.

When your baby gets bigger, at around three months, it's time to move him into a cot. Your baby should definitely be in a cot by the time he is six months old. At this age babies start to develop the ability to roll, and so will need the firm sides of a cot to prevent accidents happening.

Many parents prefer to put their babies to sleep in a cot from day one. With most modern cots you can move the mattresses up and down, changing the level depending on the age of your baby. With newborns you can put the mattress on the highest level, thus giving yourself easy access to your baby. As your baby gets older and can sit and stand up, you can lower the mattress to ensure his safety. Cots also come with a side that can drop down, so you don't have to lean over to pick your baby up.

Putting your baby down to sleep safely

To reduce the risk of cot death, follow these recommended guidelines:

- Always place your baby on his back to sleep, never on his tummy, unless advised to for medical reasons. Putting a baby to sleep on his back has been shown to reduce the risk of cot death significantly.

- Make sure you tuck your baby in firmly, ensuring his covers come no higher than his shoulders. You do not want sheets and blankets slipping over his head as this can increase the risk of cot death.

- When you tuck him into his cot or Moses basket make sure it is in a 'feet to foot' position. This is when your baby's feet are at the foot of the cot or basket, which will stop him wriggling down under his covers.

- Your baby should not be allowed to get too hot or too cold. You can test his temperature by feeling the back of his neck.

- The ideal temperature of the room your baby sleeps in is 18°C (64°F). Your baby will have difficulty regulating his body temperature so it's important that you don't let him become too hot. He should never sleep with a hot-water bottle or electric blanket, or next to a radiator, heater or fire. Keep a thermometer in his room to help you monitor the temperature.

IF YOUR BABY SLEEPS WITH YOU

You may find that night-time feeding is a lot easier if your baby sleeps in bed with you. However, there are some important points to consider before taking your baby into bed with you. Falling asleep with your baby is dangerous if you:

- or any other person in the bed is a smoker, even if you never smoke in bed

- have drunk alcohol

- have taken any drug (legal or illegal) which could make you extra sleepy

- have any illness or condition which affects your awareness of your baby

- are otherwise unusually tired to a point where you would find it difficult to respond to your baby.

The bedding

To help keep your baby safe, follow these guidelines when choosing bedding:

- The mattress in the Moses basket or cot should be firm, clean and waterproof. It should fit the Moses basket or cot well.

TOP TIP
Some parents prefer to use baby sleeping bags rather than blankets. These are quilts that you zip up around your baby and through which they can put their arms.

- There is evidence to suggest that sleeping on a second-hand mattress – one used by another baby or adult – may increase the risk of cot death, so it's best to use a brand-new mattress for each baby you have. If this is not possible make sure the mattress your baby sleeps on has a completely waterproof covering, is clean and dry, and has no tears or holes in it.

- It's best to use lightweight sheets and blankets because of a young baby's tendency to overheat.

- Do not use duvets, quilts, pillows, cot bumpers or anything 'frilly or fancy'. These are all thought to contribute to cot death: young babies are unable to lift their heads and could suffocate if in contact with these sorts of bedding.

- Always keep an eye on the temperature of your baby – reduce the number of sheets and blankets if he gets too hot.

Chapter 3

When parents say their baby 'sleeps well' or is a 'good sleeper', they usually mean their baby sleeps for several hours a night in one go without crying, disturbing his parents, or needing their help to get back to sleep. Lucky them, you might say – and indeed you would be right. Whether or not your baby is 'quiet' for big chunks of the night is in part down to luck, to the type of baby you have been blessed with. Some babies are just naturally 'better' sleepers than others. If this isn't the case with your baby, the good news is that after the first few weeks you can start to teach your baby how to be a 'good' sleeper as well. You can gently introduce routines to help him and you sleep through the night.

Night and day

One of the first things your baby needs to get his tiny little head around is the difference between night and day. Young babies have to be encouraged to develop what the rest of us take for granted: a 'diurnal' sleep pattern – the ability to sleep at night and to stay awake during the day.

Newborns, having just emerged from the womb, will have little inkling of the difference between the two. Not that they need to during their first week as they will do a lot of sleeping anyway, both during the night and the day. And at this stage it is best to be led by your baby's own rhythms and routines. As he develops and stays awake for longer periods of time he will begin to understand the difference, and there are things you can do to help with this.

Your baby will naturally pick up on what's going on around him. From very early on he will sense that when it is light there is more noise and more activity around the home. He will quickly learn that this is when the world gets going, when life around him becomes very stimulating. Don't be afraid to take your baby outdoors and expose him to daylight. But at night, when it's dark, he will sense another change in pace. Try to keep everything dark at night, when giving your baby a night-time feed or even when changing his nappy, either do it in darkness or keep the lights down low. Try not to talk to or engage with your baby by making eye contact or smiling. If you observe these differences in pace, your baby will quickly learn what's what.

> **TOP TIP**
> At night, when you have fed your baby, or changed his nappy, always put him straight back into his cot. Keep the fussing, cuddling and kissing to a minimum.

By the end of the first month you should see signs that your baby is working out the difference – at this stage he will be quieter at night. By 2–3 months, as his sleep pattern becomes more regular, you can begin to guide him into a day/night sleep routine. At 3–4 months he should be managing to sleep for several hours in a row at night.

Sleeping through the night

None of us, adults included, actually sleep through the night. As we move between our different sleep cycles we naturally wake up several times during the course of our night-time sleep *(see pages 10–11)*. The difference is that adults, and older children, can fall back to sleep unassisted, whereas young babies have to be taught how to do this. They have still to learn how to 'self soothe' – how to get to sleep without needing help in the form of feeding, cuddling or rocking *(see pages 33–35)*.

TOP TIP
It's no good trying to fit a square peg into a round hole or, to put it another way, to try and make your baby sleep like your next-door neighbour's baby. You should do what's right for you and your baby.

Sleeping through the night actually means different things to different people. When a baby is around three months old, you may hear the parents say that he is 'sleeping through the night'. Do not be fooled. What they mean is, their baby has begun sleeping for several hours in one go – say from midnight until five in the morning. These long stretches of sleep are a significant development, but before six months they are rarely for longer than five or six hours. Be assured: at this age 'sleeping through the night' does not mean lots of parents are putting their baby down to sleep at 7pm, saying goodnight, and not hearing a peep until 7am.

When do parents sleep?

Once people have enquired if your new baby is a girl or a boy, they nearly always go on to ask if you are getting enough sleep. Everyone knows lack of sleep is one of the biggest challenges for new parents; that mums and dads face nights of constant awakenings because newborns need to be cared for night and day. It's a shock, at first, to have to get out of bed several times each night to care for your baby – to feed him, change his nappy, or comfort him.

So it's not surprising that in any get-together of new parents the subject of sleep is bound to come up. Tales of disturbed nights and tiredness quickly dominate these gatherings. Random bedtimes, middle of the night upsets and early morning awakenings are much talked about. In the first few days, weeks and months it happens to everyone and it is perhaps reassuring to know that nearly every new parent is experiencing the same.

TIPS FOR COPING WITH TIREDNESS
For your sanity, it's important to find ways of coping with fatigue:

● Sleep when your baby sleeps. After all, even if you have a baby who doesn't sleep the 'average' 16 hours a day, she will still probably be sleeping 12 or so hours. It is hugely tempting to use the time that your baby sleeps during the day to do all those things you don't otherwise have time to do, or just to spend some time on your own, but if you can sometimes bring yourself to go to sleep when your baby does, you will find it really does help.

● If you have a partner, ask him to help occasionally with night feeds. You can do this even if you're breastfeeding by expressing some of your milk (that is, squeezing your breast milk out manually or using a pump) into a bottle so that your baby can still benefit from your milk. Expressing is best started after about six weeks when breastfeeding patterns are becoming established.

● Try not to organise too many things to do – keep life simple. If you're really tired, it's impossible to think straight anyway.

● Eat and exercise well. A healthy balanced diet plus exercise really will give you more energy and help you feel less tired.

● Remember that this period of sleeplessness won't last for ever. Your baby will learn to sleep through the night and you will soon feel less tired.

Sleep at different ages
Newborns: it's best to be led by your newborn baby's natural sleep rhythms. He will only sleep for 2–3 hours at a time – this is partly because his sleep cycle is short, but also because he needs feeding frequently. If he's going too long

without a feed, wake him up by gently picking up his hand, tickling his feet, changing his nappy or stroking his cheek.

This is not the time to try to introduce sleep training techniques *(see pages 20– 22)*, or, if you sense your baby does not like it, to try to get him to sleep without your help. Newborns need a lot of close physical contact, so if he becomes distressed when you put him down in his cot then do cuddle him, rock him in your arms and soothe him to sleep. He will enjoy this rocking sensation – it is similar to the type of movement he experienced while in your tummy. And if your baby falls asleep in the middle of feeding, while sucking on the bottle or breast, and seems determined to remain in this state of deep slumber – then just let him get on with it.

6 weeks–2 months: you will notice your baby developing at a rapid rate. By six weeks his sleep patterns will have matured and, because his stomach will have grown, he will be able to go longer between feeds. If you think your baby is ready to sleep or is drowsy, try putting him down in his cot while he is still awake to see if he can go to sleep unassisted. If he falls asleep during a feed, see if you can wake him up again: firstly, to make sure he finishes the feed; and secondly, to see how he copes falling asleep on his own.

3–5 months: by three months, your baby's sleep will start to become more regular and he will be able to sleep for longer periods of time. This is when you can start gradually introducing consistent routines to help him sleep well *(see pages 20– 22)*. Babies thrive on familiarity; they enjoy consistency. If a baby's days are irregular, the chances are his sleep and nights will be too.

Try making your baby's days more active by putting time aside to play with him. Feed him less on demand and more when you think he will be hungry. But, most importantly, at around this age you can start to encourage your baby to fall asleep by himself. Up until this point your baby will have associated falling asleep with you, with being fed by you or being in your arms. Now is the time to start changing these associations and attempting to 'shape' your baby's sleep patterns.

When you have finished the bedtime routine *(see pages 20–22)* and put your baby down in his cot to sleep, it's important that he's awake. That way he will learn to go to sleep by himself. If you cuddle him, rock him in your arms, lie down beside him or let him fall asleep while feeding then he will expect exactly the same treatment every time he tries to fall asleep, which could be several times a night. Babies have short sleep cycles *(see page 10–11)* and they wake briefly as they move from one cycle to the next. If during one of these awakenings your baby finds that something has changed since he first went to sleep, he will let you know. Not having the right sleep associations is the biggest cause of sleep problems for babies and young children.

From six months: by the time your baby is five months old – and certainly by the time he's six months old – he will be capable of going through the night without being fed. If he has enough nourishment during the day, and does not go to bed hungry or thirsty, he should be able to last from bedtime to breakfast without a feed. If he still wakes up for a feed at this age, try to wean him off. You should do this gradually, over a period of two weeks or more. On a night-by-night basis, slowly cut down on the length of each feed. Eventually try replacing milk with water – for both breastfed and bottle-fed babies. At this age, when babies are starting on solids, they are

COMFORTERS

If your baby starts showing an attachment to a favourite piece of sad-looking blanket or a particular soft toy, then welcome it! These 'transitional objects' will help your baby get to sleep without you standing by. He will find it very reassuring when he realises that his chosen blanket or teddy will not be going anywhere, that it is staying in his cot next to him all night.

seeking a teat or a nipple more out of comfort than hunger, using it as a means to get them off to sleep again. So now is the time to start changing those sleep associations and replacing those sleep cues.

Sleep training

At six months you can really start to shape his sleeping process. As long as he is not waking because he is sick and as long as he is gaining the right amount of weight, now is as good a time as any.

After the evening bedtime routine *(see pages 20–22)*, try tucking your baby up in his cot while he is still awake. See if he can make the transition from wakefulness to sleep by himself. In many ways this is as much a test for you as it is for him, because you need to change the way you respond to your baby. If you manage this you will have more success changing the way your baby settles and sleeps. There are various ways and means which parents use to 'sleep train' their babies. Choose the one you are most comfortable with. The important thing is to stick with it, and you can only do this if it suits you and your baby.

Controlled crying: devised by Dr Richard Ferber, a leading US paediatrician, it's also known as a 'progressive-waiting' approach. Ferber's method involves leaving your baby to 'cry it out', while constantly coming into his room to check on him as he does so. Make sure your baby is awake when you tuck him up in his cot. Say goodnight and leave the room. If he cries, come back after three minutes to soothe him, and tuck in his sheets and blankets. Keep your interaction to a minimum and do not make eye contact. Do not pick him up or take him out of his cot. Say goodnight again and leave his room. If he continues to cry come back in again after five minutes and go through the same process of tucking him in and soothing him, but not picking him up. If your baby wakes during the night repeat the exercise, working up once more from 3 to 10-minute intervals. The following night do it all again but increase the interval times to 5, 10 and 12 minutes. On the third night, increase the interval times again by a few minutes and keep doing so for successive nights until your baby is able to fall asleep on his own.

Pros

● This method can often be effective within 3–7 days.

Cons

● Many parents find it hard to see it through. Your baby may just cry a bit longer each evening to fill the interval before your return. It requires a lot of effort from parents – you could easily spend 2–3 hours each night carrying out this exercise.

Repetitive reassurance: with this method you leave your baby to settle himself, but you give him frequent reassurance throughout. Once you've put your baby down, awake in his cot, you leave the room. If he cries, go back into the room immediately, tuck him in again and reassure him. You must never pick him up, or interact with him beyond a few soothing words, but you can keep going into his room as often as you like. Keep this up until he falls asleep and do it every time he wakes up during the night.

Pros

● As you are constantly reassuring yourself and your baby it is in many ways a much gentler method. Some parents say it stops their baby getting too upset because he is seeing his parents at regular intervals.

Cons

● It can take a long time to have any effect – at least a week. It can be very frustrating because it may seem like you're never going to get there: every time your baby sees you he screams to be picked up. It takes a lot of effort from the parent; you need to spend several hours each night on this one and you may have to go in and out of your baby's bedroom many times a night.

Gradual withdrawal: the idea with this method is that you watch your baby fall asleep. Once you've settled him in his cot, you sit beside him quietly (you may want to sit and read). At no point do you make eye contact or engage with your baby. Over the next few nights, you gradually move further and further away from his cot until you are no longer in his room. The aim is only to move a little at a time – you don't move to the next position until your baby is ready.

Pros

● You can be with your baby the whole time as he learns to settle himself. It's very reassuring to a parent to be present.

Cons

● The technique takes a long time. Each time you move to a new position, you may have to stay there for 2– 3 nights before moving to the next one as you have to go at a pace your baby is comfortable with. Some babies become very upset seeing a parent in their room making no attempt to pick them up.

Common Concerns

Even when my baby sleeps I find myself watching him to check he is breathing. Is this normal?

Yes, very. You are not alone in your vigilance – many parents check their baby's breathing regularly throughout the night, especially first-time parents. If you find this reassuring then do it, especially during the first three months. In time, you will come to recognise the different noises and movements your baby makes, and it will surprise you just how noisy he can be at times.

You may also notice that there are times when your newborn appears to stop breathing all together – every so often he may 'pause' in his breathing while he sleeps – sometimes for as long as 15– 20 seconds. This is quite normal and after each pause your baby will start breathing again spontaneously. This 'periodic breathing' which is much more common in very young babies, may cause a baby to wake up and on doing so he will start breathing again. As babies develop and mature their breathing becomes more regular and these pauses happen less frequently.

I want to breastfeed my baby but am put off by constant night-time feeding. What can I do?

It is worth remembering that night-time feeding for most parents is a short-term thing. As your baby matures, as his stomach gets larger and he is able to last longer between feeds, feeding at night will become less of a feature in your life. Even by three months your baby may have begun to 'sleep through' – to manage an unbroken stretch of sleep that lasts for five or six hours. This long period of sleep usually starts after a late-night feed and lasts until the early morning – for example, from midnight until five in the morning. And by 5–6 months your baby will no longer need to be fed during the night at all. This is when he will start solid food, and as long as he is getting enough nourishment during the day there will be no physiological need for him to be fed at night. You can help wean your baby off his night-time feeds by gradually nursing him for less and less time each night. At this age babies are capable of sleeping for undisturbed stretches of 6–8 hours.

In the meantime there are several things you can do to lessen the night-time feeding load. If you have a partner, you could try sharing feeds with them. After your baby's first 4–6 weeks, once breastfeeding is well established, your partner can bottle-feed your baby at night with your expressed milk. Also, when your baby is around three months old try introducing more routine into his day and night – keeping to regular feeding, napping, and bed times. This will all help him to sleep well at night without needing to wake for a feed. Some mothers find it useful to wake their baby up for a feed when they go to bed – for example, at around 11 at night – as this sets their baby up for a good long stretch of sleep. Also at around this age try weaning your baby off you – he may be waking more for the comfort of sucking on your nipple than needing to be fed. Encourage him to suck his thumb or a dummy instead and see if that helps soothe him to sleep. *(See pros and cons of dummy and thumb sucking on pages 46–47).*

I'm a single mum and finding it hard to cope with broken nights. What can I do?
If your baby is around six months or older you could try introducing 'sleep training' *(see pages 33–35)*. Many parents find this a tough thing to do, especially in the early hours of the morning when they are very tired. It can be especially tough if you have to listen to your baby cry on your own. You may find it easier to have a friend or family member help you with the training, either to be with you while you carry it out, or, if your baby knows the other person well enough, to take turns to reassure your baby while he is in his cot. Remember the effort is worth it – it's amazing how much more positive you will feel about being a parent after a good night's sleep.

Try and catch up with your sleep during the day, either by napping when your baby naps, or seeing if another responsible adult can look after your baby while you sleep for an hour or so.

Make contact with other parents of young babies – it helps to know you are not alone and that there is a whole community out there undergoing a similar experience. *(See useful contacts page 62)*. Also, try to keep the situation in perspective – the accumulative effect of weeks of disturbed nights is undoubtedly tough on all parents, but it is often not for long. As he develops your baby will naturally, and with a bit of guidance from you, begin to sleep for longer periods each night.

Chapter 4

SLEEP PROBLEMS
How to overcome them

There are very few babies, even the champion sleepers, who get through their first year of life without a few sleep 'setbacks'. If your baby has always slept well, it might be difficult to work out why he is now not so great at it. When you are tired, in the midst of sleep-deprived nights, it might be very difficult to spot the reason for the problem and it might be very easy to think the problem is much bigger than it really is.

Illness

When your baby is ill with perhaps a cold or a tummy bug, you will know about it. You will know about it during the day, and you will know about it during the night. Your baby will seek your reassurance regularly and need to be comforted. He will need much more love and attention than usual as he snuffles and coughs his way through his first bugs.

Your baby's symptoms may be loss of appetite, a runny or blocked nose, a cough, slight feverishness, sickness or diarrhoea – all of which will affect his sleep. He will sleep more when he's ill, but it will be intermittently and not at the times you have come to expect. He will probably nap more during the day and sleep fitfully at night, waking more frequently than usual.

Young babies can become quite distressed when they have a cold and blocked nose as they have yet to learn how to breathe comfortably through their mouths. If your baby has a blocked nose, it might cause him to wake often during the night in a distressed state. He may also find it hard to feed, as sucking on a breast or bottle will be difficult for him if he is unable to breathe easily through his nose. It's therefore best to anticipate that during the few days your baby has a cold his sleeping and feeding will be unpredictable.

However, these types of minor illnesses usually last just two or three days so try not to let them have a long-term effect on any good sleep practices you have established. When your baby is ill, it's very easy to 'go backwards' with his patterns and routines. If your baby has always been happy to settle himself back to sleep *(see page 33)*, try not to resort to rocking him to sleep or letting him fall asleep in your arms, unless of course he is very distressed. And if you have managed to wean your baby off his night feeds *(see page 14– 15)*, then make sure you give him water to drink at night when he's thirsty and not milk.

During the few days that your baby is sick, it's best to put all sleep training *(see pages 33–35)* on hold and if you are about to embark on introducing new techniques, again wait until your baby is fully recovered. It will be easier on you all!

Colic

If your baby has colic, it can be very difficult to get him to settle down to sleep in the evening. Symptoms first appear when babies are around two weeks old and gradually disappear at around three months. Nobody is quite sure what causes it. Some experts believe  it's linked to a baby's immature digestion system, which is why a baby with colic behaves as if he has a stomach ache. He will draw up his knees, kick his legs and clench his fists. Others think certain babies suffer from colic because they are more sensitive, more likely to be affected by the huge amount of stimuli they encounter during their first three months, and more likely to be unable to stop crying once they start. And an increasing number of experts now think that the type of prolonged, inconsolable, crying associated with colic is an entirely normal part of human development. That there is nothing 'wrong' with your baby when he is wailing like this and that he is not actually trying to let you know that there is. In fact all your baby may be doing is merely venting – crying for the sake of it and finding it difficult to stop crying once he's started.

The main symptom of colic is crying – on and off for several hours, or over one long stretch. These bouts of crying usually start in the late afternoon or early evening after a feed, and can go on until eleven or twelve at night when your baby (and you) fall into an exhausted sleep. A baby with colic is very difficult to soothe. You can walk around with him, rock him gently, let him suck for comfort, try to feed him, but at

TOP TIP

It can help to keep a sleep diary, to note down when your baby is sleeping and when he is waking, when he is feeding and, after he starts solids, what he is feeding on. This can help you get to the root of a sleep problem and may be useful if you want to discuss the problem with your health visitor.

times he will be inconsolable. There are no proven cures for colic – some parents find that giving their baby a dummy *(see pages 46–47)* helps and there are remedies available from pharmacists.

Colic will make bedtime routines, late-afternoon naps, or any attempt to put your baby down in his cot to settle by himself, difficult. But do not give up on them altogether – you do not want to get into too many bad habits early on. And what all experts do agree on is that colic is a short-term problem; by four months your baby will be over it, and it rarely affects a baby's weight gain or general health.

TOP TIP
Many parents find teething rings or teething gels, available from pharmacists, do help to ease their baby's discomfort.

Reflux

This is also linked to the immaturity of your baby's digestive system. It is effectively 'heartburn' and will affect your baby's sleep – he might find it hard to go to sleep and, when he's got to sleep, be awakened by pain. Reflux is caused when a baby regurgitates his feed repeatedly. If you think your baby is suffering from reflux, seek medical advice.

As with colic, the majority of babies outgrow reflux, and as long as a baby is putting on weight and otherwise healthy, it is not thought of as a serious problem.

Teething

A few babies are born with teeth, but for most others their first ones will start to appear between the ages of five and nine months (but if there is still no sign of a first tooth by the time your baby is a year old, there is no need to worry). Teething affects babies differently. Some babies seem hardly bothered by it, while others find it hard going and can be irritable. Teething can cause increased dribbling, swollen gums, a desire to suck more than usual, and occasionally a slightly raised temperature.

That said, a lot of sleep problems are, wrongly, blamed on teething. It's true that discomfort from teething can affect sleep, but it will only be for a few nights, not weeks.

Food intolerance

Not all foods agree with every child, so when you start your baby on solids, at around six months, do monitor how he reacts to them. Certain foods can cause an adverse reaction in some children. The symptoms vary widely: from eczema and asthma to diarrhoea, to maybe just being a bit irritable. However, they all have the potential to affect your baby's sleep. If you suspect your child has an intolerance, an 'allergy' to something, it's best to cut that food out from his diet and perhaps reintroduce it when he is older. If in doubt, consult with your doctor or health visitor.

Separation anxiety

You might be surprised when, at around seven or eight months, your 'perfect sleeper' of a baby starts waking up during the night. You have managed to get him off his night feeds, he always settles himself back to sleep again, his routine of daytime and night-time sleeping is progressing nicely – so why has he started waking up in the night? The reason is often more psychological than physical. At around this age babies start exhibiting signs of 'separation anxiety' – they show quite clearly that they really don't like it when you are not around. They cry when you leave the room, they are more clingy than usual, they literally do not want you out of their sight. And it's

around this age that they show they really don't like strangers – they often cry if they are picked up by someone they do not know.

This is a very normal part of your baby's development – it shows he is becoming more aware of who he is, and who you are, and that there might just be a difference! But it also means he could become difficult to settle. He may want you there by his side and become distressed if this does not happen fast. Any separation from you will cause your baby anxiety – whether it happens during the day or night. This anxiety may well last for several months, so you will have to be patient. If you do not want to be with him every time he settles himself to sleep again, then maybe try a sleep training technique, like gradual withdrawal *(see pages 34– 35).*

A 'sucky' baby

In the same way that some babies eat and sleep better than others, some are naturally more 'sucky' than others; your baby might find the act of sucking very soothing and that it helps to send him off to sleep. This is fine if your baby is young and still needs to be fed at night, as he will be easily comforted by sucking on a teat or a nipple. But at around six months old, your baby will be physiologically capable of lasting from supper until breakfast without a feed, so you may want to change this sleep association. This is a good time to not only wean him off his middle-of-the- night feed, but also to wean him off you. A dummy can sometimes help with this, although there are some disadvantages to using one *(see pages 46– 47).*

TOP TIP
Learn to appreciate the early morning: like adults, some babies are larks, while others are owls. Accept that you may simply have a naturally early riser on your hands.

Early risers

Oh the joys of the early morning – little did you know, before you had a baby, just how much went on in the world between five and six in the morning. If you are able to work out why your baby is waking up so early, you may be able to do something about it and maybe even have a bit of a lie-in.

● Your baby may be waking a little earlier each day because he is hungry and

WHEN THE CLOCKS GO BACK

When you have a baby you may not get that extra hour to sleep. Babies are adaptable, but not that adaptable. When the clocks are switched from winter to summertime, it's best to start your baby off at his new bedtime straight away. Most children manage to adjust to the hour's difference within a week.

expects a feed. Try to delay this feed as much as possible – especially with babies over six months.

● How your baby sleeps during the day will affect the way he sleeps at night. So make sure he has enough naps *(see pages 13–17)*. An overtired baby may not sleep well.

● Make sure your baby has a suitable amount of activity during the day and that he has plenty of stimulation.

● Check you are not putting your baby to bed too early – especially as he gets older. If you put your twelve-month-old baby to sleep at six in the evening you will be lucky if he wakes up much after six the next morning. Try putting him to bed a little later each night, but be aware that this doesn't always make a difference.

● After about three months, babies become much more aware of their environment. So check your baby's room is not too warm or too cold *(see page 24)*. If it is getting light early in the morning, consider putting up some black-out blinds to see if that helps your baby sleep for longer.

● Don't rush straight in to help your baby when you hear him stir; wait to see

TOP TIP
Wherever you are, even if it's the other side of the world, try starting your baby off on local time straight away. It might take him a few days to make the switch or as much as a week in some time zones, but you might find that he makes the 'switch' quicker than you!

PROS AND CONS OF DUMMIES AND THUMB SUCKING

DUMMIES

Pros

- Babies find sucking very comforting, which is one of the reasons why they often fall asleep at the end, or during, a feed. Many mothers find a dummy provides the same type of comfort and helps a baby settle to sleep on his own.
- If your baby manages not to lose his dummy while sleeping, he is more likely to 'keep' sleeping and not wake up fully and cry between sleep cycles.
- Dummies are very safe: it is impossible for a baby to choke on or swallow one. The teat of the dummy is made of silicone, rubber or latex and is attached to a plastic mouth shield.
- Dummies are easy to keep clean and can be sterilised in the same way as the teat of a bottle.
- There is some evidence to suggest that the use of a dummy may help protect against cot death, but the reason why has yet to be fully established.

Cons

- Encouraging your baby to use a dummy may affect your chances of breastfeeding successfully, especially if your baby starts using one during his first six weeks. When your baby sucks, he stimulates your breasts to produce milk. If you give him a dummy to suck on instead of your breast this may hinder the production of breast milk, which can cause feeding problems.
- Some experts believe that using a dummy can cause 'nipple confusion' – that your young baby may find it difficult to swap between your nipple and the teat of a dummy.
- Studies show that babies who use dummies regularly are more likely to be weaned earlier; they are breastfed for a shorter period of time compared to babies who use dummies infrequently or not at all.

- Once your baby gets the hang of his dummy, it may be very difficult to get him to give up the habit.
- Although a dummy may help your baby soothe himself to sleep, if he loses it in his cot at night it will unsettle him. He may wake up and cry and he may not stop crying until you come running to retrieve the dummy for him.
- Frequent use of a dummy has been linked to an increased susceptibility to ear and stomach infections in young babies.
- It is thought that dummy use may affect speech development. 'Babbling' is an important part of learning to talk, but if your baby regularly has a dummy in his mouth he may not be able to do this as often as he would do if he did not use a dummy.
- Long-term use of a dummy may cause dental problems. Continuous sucking over a number of years may distort your child's 'bite' – when the upper and lower teeth do not meet properly.

THUMB SUCKING

Pros

- It's difficult to lose this comforter in the middle of the night or in a shopping centre.
- Some babies need little in the way of introduction to their thumb.

Cons

- Thumbsucking is more likely than dummies to cause problems with teeth alignment.
- You can take a dummy away but there's not much you can do to hide a thumb.

if he's happy on his own for a while, or even manages to go back to sleep. When he's six months old, you can put some toys in his cot to see if he will occupy himself with them for half an hour or so, therefore giving you a bit of extra sleep.

Swaddling your newborn

'Swaddling' your baby means wrapping him up tight in a thin shawl or blanket in such a way that his arms are kept firmly by his sides, with only his head uncovered. It may sound strange, but in many cultures around the world babies are swaddled from birth and millions of parents believe it to be a very effective way of helping them to sleep.

TOP TIP
As your baby gets older try leaving his arms outside the blanket when you swaddle him. By just wrapping the blanket around his body and legs, his hands, fingers and thumbs are free so he can put them in his mouth to suck and soothe himself.

Young babies – especially newborns – have a very strong Moro reflex. This is what causes them to twitch and jerk, often quite dramatically, while sleeping. These sudden movements often startle infants, causing them to wake up. By swaddling a baby, you are lessening the effect of these involuntary actions and some experts believe that by copying the restrictive conditions in the womb you are helping your baby feel more secure.

How to swaddle your baby:

1. Make a triangle shape out of a thin shawl or blanket and put it down on a flat surface.

2. While your baby is still awake, lay him on the blanket. Make sure his neck is level with the longest edge of your triangle and that his head is the only part of his body not resting on the blanket.

3. Take hold of the right-hand corner of the blanket. Bring it across your baby's body, tucking it tightly under his right arm.

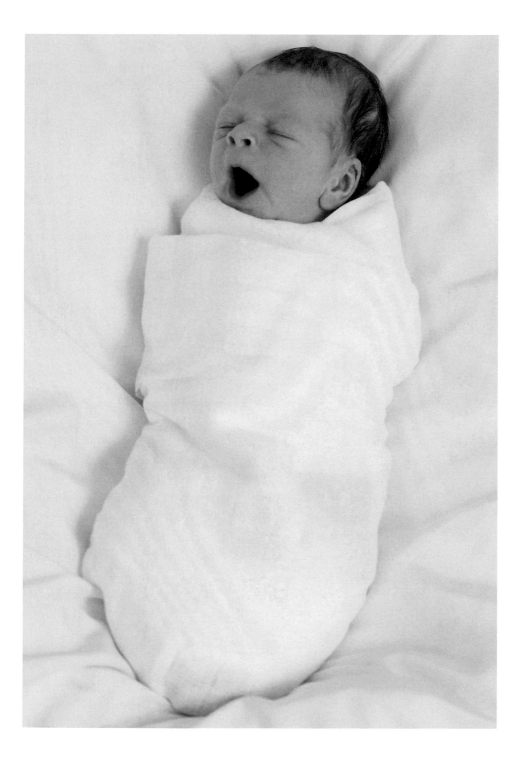

4. Take the left corner and fold it across your baby. Make sure his left arm is wrapped up in the blanket, and then tuck it underneath him.

5. Tuck the end of the blanket firmly under your baby's feet.

Common concerns

How safe is it for my baby to sleep in his car seat?

It should be fine for your baby to sleep in his car seat for short periods of time, with you close by to keep an eye on him. But it's important to remember that car seats are not meant to be permanent sleeping places for babies. Being in a semi-upright position for long periods of time can place a strain on your baby's developing spine, and if your baby slumps over with his head down it can restrict his breathing. Recent research suggests that placing babies of one month or under in a sitting position for long periods of time can make them more susceptible to breathing difficulties.

Therefore it's best to break up long car journeys and take your baby out of his car seat regularly – putting him on his back or holding him upright for a while. Remember the safest sleeping position for your baby is on his back, on a firm mattress, so if you are not in the car always take him out of his car seat and put him in his cot. Never let him sleep all night in a car seat.

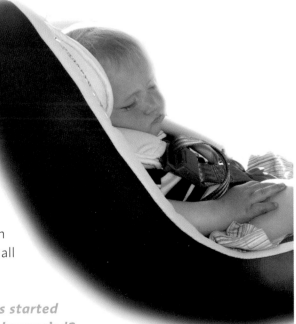

My two-month-old baby has started 'snoring' in his sleep – should I be worried?

It's always a bit of a shock to hear a tiny baby snoring or snorting in his sleep; it's amazing how something so small can produce so much noise while he slumbers. However, it is quite common for babies to make a variety of snuffling-type noises in their sleep. Newborns tend to be 'noisy breathers' because their airways are still very narrow and often filled with mucus which vibrates with each intake of breath. This is particularly so if they have a cold.

TOP TIP
Research suggests that babies exposed to plenty of daylight are more likely to have a better night's sleep. This is especially true if they are exposed to light during the early afternoon either by being outdoors or by being put near a window at home. Exposure to daylight will help with the development of their sleep patterns and rhythms.

In most cases these early bouts of snoring are short-lived – the snoring subsides as a baby matures, his airways grow, and the whole business of living becomes generally easier for him. But if your baby's snoring is persistent or especially loud, if it does not lessen as he gets older, or if you are in any way worried about it then do consult with your health visitor or GP. They will check for problems and perhaps refer you to an ear, nose and throat specialist.

My three month old baby doesn't seem to sleep as much as other babies and he is not sleeping for any long stretches during the night. He is still waking up every three hours or so and expecting a feed. Should I be worried?
Not at all. Babies develop in different ways for many reasons. Your baby may be a 'hungry' baby - one that needs to eat a lot and often; he may be a 'sensitive' baby - one that craves more comforting and holding than others; or he may be a 'sucky' baby - one that enjoys the comfort of a nipple or teat to soothe him. If your baby is putting on the right amount of weight and appears to be alert and happy during the day then there is no reason to worry about him waking frequently at night. However, if you are finding this very tiring and it is getting too much for you then you may want to think about changing your baby's sleep associations and introducing a sleep routine *(see pages 33-35)*. But if you are one of those people who copes well with interrupted nights there really is nothing to worry about.

Chapter 5

SPECIAL CIRCUMSTANCES
Babies who need extra help to sleep

In some circumstances the normal sleep strategies described may not be effective or take longer to work. You may need extra help and support, and in some cases specialist help. What will not help you at all is to compare and contrast – to swap notes with other parents of similar aged babies about how their infants are sleeping. Remember every baby is different and sleep patterns will vary enormously – especially for those babies who may take longer to reach developmental milestones. To help prevent, or lessen the impact of your baby having a persistent sleep problem, it is best to seek professional guidance as early as possible.

Twins

If your twins are identical, they will probably be very similar in the way they sleep – their rhythms and patterns and their ability to settle. If they are fraternal twins, the similarities will be less strong; they will be the same as for all siblings. And this, as any mother of more than one child will tell you, can mean your babies are actually not very similar at all! One twin may weigh more, eat more and sleep more. The other may be lighter, fussier and much more active. One twin could be a very good sleeper, who slips effortlessly into predictable long periods of sleep. The other may be the opposite: he may seek far more cuddling, rocking and holding to get him to sleep, and he may spend a lot more time awake compared with his sibling.

Despite these differences, when it comes to sleep, you need to aim to make your twins' sleep schedules as similar as possible. Life will be so much easier if you do. You need rest and sleep as much as your new babies do, and you can only do this when your twins are asleep. The most common situation for parents of twins is that one parent is looking after two babies most of the time. Only in the evenings and at night can the other parent help out. Remember you have

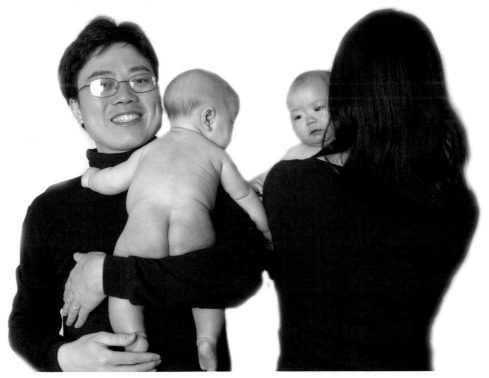

double the caring to do, so it's important to look after yourself as well. So right from the beginning try to encourage good sleep habits – from the first week and definitely by six weeks.

TOP TIP
Synchronising your babies' feeds is key to making sure you all get more sleep at the same time. Try to give your babies their last feed at the same time every evening before tucking them up in their cots. During the night, if one of them wakes for a feed, wake the other/s and see if they will also take a feed.

1. Aim to start a relaxed bedtime routine *(see pages 20–22)* during your twins' first week. It doesn't need to consist of much, just a feed and a nappy change, but if you keep it to the same time every day it will help everyone – you, as much as your babies. Set a time each evening when you want their actual bedtime to be and work backwards from that. Your twins will quickly come to enjoy the preparations for bed, especially time spent in a warm bath.

2. You will be doing yourself a huge favour if you encourage your twins to settle themselves to sleep, to be able to 'self soothe' *(see pages 31–33)*. Putting a lot of effort into settling a baby to sleep is just not possible if you have to care for two of them on your own. So do not spend too long cuddling and comforting your babies before tucking them up each night. Try putting them down in their Moses baskets *(see page 23)* or cots when they are drowsy, before they are in a deep sleep.

3. If one, or both of your babies cry, do not immediately go and pick them up. Try leaving them for a few minutes to see how they cope. If their crying becomes less intense, hold back a bit to see if they will fall asleep.

4. Twins are used to being around each other – when they are young they are unlikely to be disturbed by the crying of their sibling. In the same way that a young baby can sleep through an alarm going off, they can easily manage to ignore the screeching of their sibling. So if one is crying do not immediately pick him up out of worry that they will disturb the other – many parents say that one twin is often oblivious to the crying of his sibling.

5. If, after six months you want to introduce sleep training *(see pages 33– 35),* then you may find it easier to put one twin in a separate bedroom.

6. It will be much easier on everyone if your twins sleep and wake up at the same time – especially in the morning. So from around six weeks old, when your babies' sleep patterns will be more developed, try to synchronise their sleep/wake cycles. As soon as one baby wakes up, gently wake the other one up as well *(see pages 30– 31).* If you start their day off together, you have a much better chance of ending it at the same time.

Special care babies

Some babies need more care than others: those born prematurely, babies who have had a difficult and complicated birth, and those with a disability. During their first year, and perhaps for longer, they will need extra help to reach key developmental milestones. Their progress may appear slower than with other newborns, and their feeding and sleeping patterns very different. You should not let these differences stop you introducing good sleep habits. As long as you are prepared for it to take a bit longer than usual, there is no reason why you shouldn't try, and there is no reason, especially in the case of premature babies, why you shouldn't be successful.

Premature babies: a premature baby or a 'pre-term' baby is one that is born before 37 weeks gestation. A 'full-term' baby is born anywhere between 38– 42 weeks. The earlier a baby is born before his due date, the more care he usually needs. A premature baby has to do more developing outside the ideal conditions of the womb, so has some 'catching up' to do compared to a full-term baby.

Part of this catching up includes sleep: a pre-term baby's sleep patterns are behind those of his peers. Premature babies sleep for more hours of the day – an average of 18 hours over a 24-hour period, compared to a full-term baby who sleeps an average of 16 hours over a 24-hour period. A pre-term baby's sleep is 'lighter': 80 per cent of the sleep he experiences is REM sleep *(see page 8).* He will sleep for much shorter periods of time, be prone to night wakings for longer and need to be fed more frequently than a full-term baby. He may also take longer to work out the difference between day and night *(see page 28),* especially if he's been in a special care baby unit.

However, your pre-term baby's sleep patterns will settle in time. He will eventually start sleeping for longer and longer periods, but it might take him

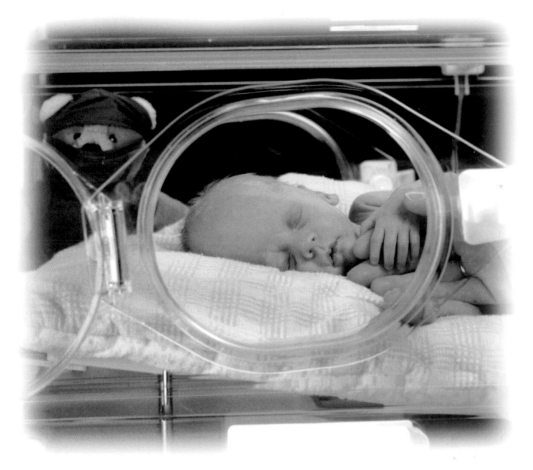

months to do this rather than weeks. You can start introducing your baby to good sleep habits from his due date: start a bedtime routine, respect the difference between night and day, and, as he develops, encourage him to settle in exactly the same way as you would a full-term baby.

A baby with a disability: a baby's disability or certain medical conditions may cause a sleep problem. Introducing good sleep habits when he is very young may not be realistic, and in some cases it may be irrelevant. Also, parents may be reluctant to encourage practices such as self-soothing *(see page 33– 35)* with such especially vulnerable babies. But if your GP or health visitor advises it, then it is worth attempting the basics and persevering with whatever progress you make – you may find your baby really benefits from routine and schedules. It's best to get specialist advice on when your baby may be ready to start on these routines.

● For some babies with a disability, learning from experience is often difficult. Your baby may not pick up on sleep cues and routines. 'Settling down' each night may mean very little to him and sorting out day from night could be particularly confusing. Be prepared for this, but do not let it stop you trying.

● If your baby has Down's syndrome he may have breathing difficulties, which will affect his sleep. Your health visitor will advise you on what to do or you could seek support from a specialist organisation.

● Babies who are later diagnosed with autistic spectrum disorders can have great difficulty settling. Your baby may wake more frequently than others, and will be more likely to wake early in the morning. It's best to seek professional advice.

● The sleep cycles and patterns of a baby suffering from brain damage may be affected. Your baby may not develop an ability to sleep well in the same ways as other babies of a similar age, and when he's older he may need medication to help him. Your doctor and health visitor will be able to advise you on how to help your baby, or you could contact a specialist sleep clinic.

Fussy babies

'Fussy' babies are called a lot of different names for example, sensitive, high needs, anxious. They tend to need more hands-on care than other babies – they need more reassurance, more physical contact, more touching and carrying, more rocking and motion. If they don't get what they want, they cry. Often parents find the only way to keep them happy is to keep them close and carry them around all the time, in a sling or in their arms. This is not the type of baby who can be put down for long, or who finds self-soothing *(see pages 33– 35)* easy.

Not surprisingly, these types of babies do end up with sleep problems, possibly because they are so sensitive and react so strongly to being left on their own, and possibly because their parents reinforce their behaviour by running to them every time they cry. If you have a sensitive baby and are trying to encourage good sleep habits it might help to remember that crying is a very natural part of being a baby and sometimes babies cry a lot for no apparent reason: they are healthy, putting on weight, well fed, and not overtired. Life usually gets a lot easier for these babies as they get older – they do become more independent and robust.

Common concerns

Is it safe to let my twins sleep in the same cot together?

As long as you stick to the guidelines for sleeping safely then yes, 'co-bedding' is absolutely fine. Research shows that it is no more risky for multiples to sleep side by side in the same cot than to sleep separately. Just make sure they are well tucked in, lying on their backs with their feet at the end of the cot. Some parents say their twins actually sleep better when together – they settle more easily. And you can see why this may be so - multiples are very used to being near each other, they've spent several months in close proximity while developing in the womb. But it's important to remember that there will come a time when your twins start disturbing each other or will be too big to share the same cot and separating them when they are a few months old, after they have got used to sleeping next to each other, often requires more effort than separating them at birth.

Conclusion

Studies show that between a fifth and a third of parents of pre-school children say their child has a 'sleep problem'. A lot of these 'problems' begin when their children are babies; their issues start out very small, but can go on for several years. In many ways the issue is actually with the parent and not with the baby; it's about the way the parent reacts when their baby goes to sleep and wakes up. So sorting out your baby's sleep problem is really about you adopting the 'right' response to your baby's behaviour. As a new parent you are often on as steep a learning curve as your baby! But if you can help your baby to sleep well from just a few months old, then you will be helping the whole family to sleep well for years to come.

USEFUL ORGANISATIONS

The Association for Post-Natal Illness
Helpline:020 7386 0868
Website: www.apni.org
Provides support to mothers suffering from post-natal illness and works towards increasing public awareness of the illness.

Association of Breastfeeding Mothers (ABM)
Counselling hotline: 08444 122949
Website: abm.me.uk
A mutual support group for breastfeeding mothers. Puts mothers in touch with each other and provides information and advice.

Bliss
t 020 7378 1122, f 020 7403 0673
Parent Support Helpline:
FREEPHONE 0500 618140
Website: www.bliss.org.uk
A national organisation working for special care babies and their families. It provides information and
support for all those caring for premature and sick babies.

Cry-sis
Helpline: 08451 228669
Website: www.cry-sis.org.uk
A charity providing self-help and support to families with excessively crying, sleepless and demanding babies.

Foundation for the Study of Infant Deaths (FSID)
Website: www.fsid.org.uk
Helpline: 020 7233 2090
Offers support and education to parents and professionals on reducing the risk of Sudden Infant Death Syndrome (SIDS).

Gingerbread
Helpline: 0800 018 5026
Website: www.gingerbread.org.uk
Provides support services and a self-help network to ensure lone-parent families do not have to face challenges alone

Home Start
Phone: 0116 233 9955
Website: www.home-start.org.uk/
An organisation that has a network of 15,000 trained parent volunteers who support parents struggling to cope. This can be for many different reasons: post-natal illness, disability, bereavement, the illness of a parent or child, or social isolation.

Meet-A-Mum Association (MAMA)
Helpline: +44 0845 120 3746 - 7pm - 10pm Weekdays Only
http://www.mama.co.uk/
Provides friendship and support to all mothers and mothers-to-be, especially those feeling lonely or isolated after the birth of a baby or moving to a new area. By attending a local MAMA group, mums become part of a network of women wanting to make new friends and support each other through good times and bad.

The National Childbirth Trust
General enquiry line: 0870 770 3236
Breastfeeding line: 0870 444 8708
(9am to 6pm, seven days a week)
To talk to a qualified breastfeeding counsellor about breastfeeding.
Website: www.nct.org.uk
Antenatal and postnatal classes giving information and help to mothers, including help with breastfeeding.

Parentline Plus
Phone: 0808 800 2222
Website: www.parentlineplus.org.uk/
A national charity that works for, and with, parents.

Tamba
Phone: 0870 770 3305
Website: www.tamba.org.uk
A nationwide UK charity providing information and mutual support networks for families of twins, triplets and more.

INDEX

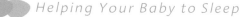
INDEX

1 3 5 7 9 10 8 6 4 2

Published in 2008 by Vermilion, an imprint of Ebury Publishing

A Random House Group Company

The Random House Group Limited Reg. No. 954009

Addresses for companies within the Random House Group can be found at
www.randomhouse.co.uk

A CIP catalogue record for this book is available from the British Library

The Random House Group Limited makes every effort to ensure that the papers used in our books are made from trees that have been legally sourced from well-managed and credibly certified forests. Our paper procurement policy can be found on www.rbooks.co.uk/environment

To buy books by your favourite authors and register for offers visit www.rbooks.co.uk

Printed and bound in Singapore by Tien Wah Press

ISBN 9780091923457

Please note that conversions to imperial weights and measures are suitable equivalents and not exact.

The information given in this book should not be treated as a substitute for qualified medical advice; always consult a medical practitioner. Neither the author nor the publisher can be held responsible for any loss or claim arising out of the use, or misuse, of the suggestions made or the failure to take medical advice.